TEACHING WITH HEART

MAKING STUDENT CONNECTIONS THAT COUNT

JANE BLOMSTRAND

B&P Books
www.BooksNPieces.com

A REQUEST FROM THE AUTHOR

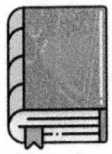

After you have read this book PLEASE take a moment to leave me a brief, honest review. You may do so where you purchased the book (Amazon, Barnes and Noble...)

Thank you,

Jane Blomstrand,
Author

To all the students out there who hope
to have a "GOOD" teacher.....

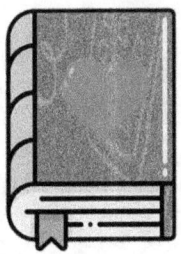

CONTENTS

INTRODUCTION

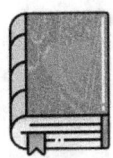

> "**All kids need is a little help, a little hope, and somebody who believes in them.**" ~ *Magic Johnson*

A new teacher once made an insightful comment to me. Teaching was a second career for him. While working as a scientist for twenty-five years, he developed a passion for his field and knew it backward and forward. Teaching what he loved and creating an appreciation for science among his students excited him.

He told me, "I planned for my classes all summer, I created lessons for the first few months of school, I put up interesting and colorful bulletin boards, I worked my tail off to be ready. I was as prepared as anyone could be. *And then, the students arrived.*"

Teaching is a challenging occupation. It's one thing to follow the curriculum and plan thoughtful, interesting, and instructional lessons. But engaging students is where the magic happens. We need to get to know them and what they need, and we need to engage them; we need to cultivate relationships with them.

Educators begin teaching wanting to excel at their craft and teach engaged students eager to soak up knowledge. It's exciting to think about. But there's another side to this coin; students are human beings full of emotions and their own thoughts. They bring different histories into the classroom. As teachers, we need to listen to their thoughts and ideas, respect them, and help them take ownership of their education. It's important to get to know and understand them.

University programs have courses in classroom management and creating positive environments. Still, many teachers never anticipate the multitude of personalities they will encounter in their classrooms, the different attention levels of their students, what backgrounds they bring into the classroom, and whether they will be interested in the subject matter.

A teacher might love science and expect their students will also, but it's the relationships that develop between student and teacher that make the difference in whether students are engaged or not. We have known this for a long time. It's nothing new. It's just sometimes, in the vast expanse of teaching responsibilities, we forget this very important aspect. Our experience during the Covid-19 pandemic reminded us of the importance of making that personal connection with students. Educators are now focusing more on the socio-emotional piece in teaching. But getting to know a student takes time and time is a precious commodity among teachers. Elementary teachers have a multitude of subjects to teach. Secondary teachers have 100-150 students to teach, and they only see them for about 45-50 minutes per day. School districts have tried to help teachers in this domain by implementing different programs.

There is the Multi-Tiered Systems of Support (MTSS) framework and many Social-Emotional Learning (SEL) programs to choose from, like PBIS (Positive Behavioral Interventions and Supports), Mindful Life, Character Strong; the list goes on and on. These programs have wonderful messages and strategies that teach our students and the adults on campus about caring, empathy, and inclusiveness. They help create a positive school culture and climate. But what happens in the classroom interactions between teacher and student is what makes the difference, and for meaningful learning to take place, the student needs to feel the teacher cares about them, and the way to do that is to take the time to get to know them.

Just the other day, my fourteen-year-old grandson described his math teacher to me. He said Mr. X was a good teacher. I asked him what made his math teacher a good teacher. He told me, "Mr. X cares about us. He asks us questions and listens to our answers. He gets to know us." There are so many facets of teaching to think about, and connecting with students is probably the most important.

Focusing on building relationships doesn't mean that we let up on our academic expectations, it just means we pay attention to both dimensions. As we are developing relationships with and engaging our students, we should also expect and help them to do their best work and take ownership of their learning.

I hope the information in this book will reinforce the importance of getting to know your students. Perhaps it will augment ideas you already have in place building these relationships or provide new ideas for you to incorporate into your classroom interactions with your students.

~ *Jane Blomstrand*

DEVELOP A RELATIONSHIP
WITH YOUR STUDENTS!

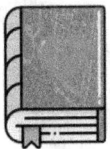

> **"Classroom management is not about having the right rules, it's about having the right relationships."** *~Danny Steele*

 $\mathcal{I}$ recently had the privilege of participating in "Teacher of the Year" visitations for the local County Office of Education. Our team observed teachers in many schools in several districts. We visited elementary, middle, and high school classrooms. After each observation, we met with the individual teacher and asked a series of questions. One of the questions we asked was, "To what do you attribute your success as a teacher?" In every interview, whether it was kindergarten, high school, or special education, included in the teacher's answer was, "I build relationships with my students."

A positive relationship with a student provides a comfortable space in which they can learn, increases student motivation to learn, and improves student behavior. Along with knowing the curriculum they will teach and how to manage a classroom full of energetic students effectively, teachers should also consider the value of building relationships with their students. Students need to know their teacher cares about them and their learning; they need to see if the teacher believes they "can" learn and will support them in that process. We need to build trust and create a safe environment in which students can learn. To do this, we need to listen, understand, engage, respect, and expect our students to succeed.

During the Covid-19 pandemic, I had a conversation with an 8th grader whose graduation consisted of the graduates being driven up in front of the school by their families in cars to receive their certificates. At first, she was disappointed about not being able to have the traditional graduation ceremony she had seen for her sister. Surprisingly, after her graduation, she told me that she felt it was more personal than walking across a stage because all her teachers were out front greeting each car as they passed by. The teachers talked to each student, said nice personal things about them, and gave them compliments in front of their family members. She felt very respected and valued. She said she felt part of a caring community.

Her comments caused me to think of a term I heard a while back: Ubuntu. It's an old philosophy that originated in the continent of Africa. It became known in the West mainly through the writings of Desmond Tutu, who won the Nobel Peace Prize for his opposition to apartheid in South Africa. According to Wikipedia, "...at its most basic, Ubuntu can be translated as 'human kindness,' but its meaning is much bigger in scope than that; it embodies the ideas of connection, community, and mutual caring for all. It's a way of living that begins with the premise that "I am" because "We are." That one's sense of self is shaped by your relationships with other people. We are human because we participate in relationships. No one is an island; everything we do, good or bad, influences those around us, including our family, our friends, and society. My humanity is tied to yours.

I've been reading more about Ubuntu lately and have concluded that we can embrace this premise in our schools and our work with youth. Teachers, coaches, and everyone who works with young people should embody the concept of Ubuntu in their everyday practice, implementing its deeply rooted virtues of respect and compassion and building relationships with others.

I think of a recent situation involving a young boy I know named Sam. Sam played on a baseball team. One day, he was at second base in a tournament and didn't position himself as the coach had instructed. When the batter hit the ball, it went through the infield, where Sam was instructed to be, and continued into the outfield, causing a run to score for the other team. After the game was over, the coach came into the dugout and reprimanded Sam in front of his teammates for not being in the correct position. Tears formed in Sam's eyes, at which point the coach demanded, "What are the tears for?" Sam responded, "It doesn't feel very good when you're yelling at me about what a terrible player I am." The coach became upset, telling Sam he was disrespectful and that if he kept this up, he may not be on the team anymore. Sam went home after the game, dejected. He talked through the situation with his parents and, that night, sent a text to his coach apologizing for his behavior. The following day, Sam and his parents drove 1-½ hours for the tournament's final two games. His parents had prepared him for the fact that he would probably be benched for a few innings as a consequence of his transgression. It turned out that Sam was benched for both games that day, and he never played an inning.

Luckily, Sam's parents, without knowing it, practiced Ubuntu when they helped him deal with and try to understand that discipline. He took the high road, handled the situation maturely, and moved on.

Imagine a different scenario, one where the coach pulled Sam aside and talked to him about the consequences for his team of not playing his position correctly, the importance of teamwork, and how everyone needs to do their part for the good of the whole team—talked to him using compassion and the concept of Ubuntu. That conversation would have been a more valuable learning experience for Sam and taught him an important lesson about teamwork that he could carry into the future.

It's so easy to point out the mistakes of others, particularly our students. But how often do we take the time to provide positive feedback to students when they do what is expected? There is a term I recently learned called Ratio of Interactions (ROI). ROI means making a conscious effort to interact with a student more frequently when they are doing something appropriate instead of something inappropriate. On any school site, attention from adults is sought after by students more often than not. Much to our surprise, many students would rather be yelled at by an adult than ignored. Increasing your positive interactions with students and calling out the good they do has lasting benefits for both students and adults.

According to Christopher Emdin, an author and educator, another approach for getting to know a student is to use his "2 x 10" strategy. First, select a student you are struggling to connect with. Engage that student on any topic for two minutes, then continue having those two-minute conversations about any subject for ten consecutive days. His research indicates there is a significant improvement in that student's behavior. When a student knows you care enough about him/her to engage in conversation with them, it lets them know you respect them, helps to build trust, and provides a safe environment for learning.

During these conversations and other times, talk to students about what's important to them and ask them questions to learn more about what interests them and motivates them. If you sense something is troubling them, ask if they are okay. If they are working on an assignment, ask them what their focus is? What might their next steps be? What is challenging or tricky about the assignment? Do they need any help in completing the assignment?

Make a list of several things you know about each of your students—you may be surprised to learn there are some you know little about. You may have them or their parents complete a Student Strengths Survey. If the student is old enough, they can complete it themselves. These surveys ask questions such as: What are two strengths I have? What is one success I am proud of? What are some words that describe me? This lets the students know you are interested in them and provides valuable information for you to employ when planning lessons or managing your classroom.

Some behaviors detrimental to forming a positive relationship with a student and very important to acknowledge and avoid as the adult in the room are: sarcasm, holding grudges, and embarrassing students in front of others. Conversations about missing assignments, grades, etc., should be held one-on-one and in private. Holding grudges and "teaching them a lesson" are non-productive strategies that diminish trust and create a hostile environment. Sarcasm, defined in the dictionary, is "a sharp and often satirical or ironic utterance designed to cut or give pain." It has no place when trying to cultivate a positive relationship with students.

When students receive praise a positive occurrence happens in the brain, and it releases dopamine, which makes the student feel good. This can create a cycle. When the student feels good they are more motivated to feel that way again, which hopefully results in more positive interactions and increased learning taking place.

Taking the time to build a relationship with a student is fundamental to academic success. Feeling good about themselves at school helps students feel more supported and safer in the classroom and results in more engagement and increased learning.

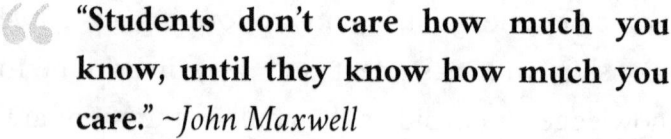 **"Students don't care how much you know, until they know how much you care."** *~John Maxwell*

MINDFULLY LISTEN TO YOUR STUDENTS!

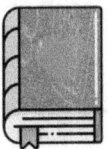

> "**Listen first to understand, then to be understood.**" ~Stephen Covey

*P*art of building a relationship is to hear what others have to say. To hear another, you need to listen. The dictionary definition of 'listen' is to pay attention to sound and to hear something with thoughtful attention.

Have you heard the acronym W.A.I.T? I recently heard about it on a podcast. It resonated with me. W.A.I.T *stands for Why Am I Talking*? I believe W.A.I.T could be the partner to listen. When we're talking, we can't listen, and if we think we are, we could be fooling ourselves. There are many circumstances I find myself in where I should be asking myself W.A.I.T., *Why Am I Talking?*

One example is when a group of teachers and I meet in the faculty room. We get into some serious, animated conversations. It's easy for one of us to bring up a subject and another to start talking about their experience with that subject. This unknowingly removes the conversation from the person who started the topic. No one does it intentionally, but because we can be so passionate, excited, or incensed about something, we want to share our thoughts and experiences with it. In doing so, we hijack the conversation from the person who brought it up, and they may never end up expressing their original thoughts.

Have you ever been in a one-on-one conversation with someone when you're talking, and they responded with a comment that didn't connect with what you were saying? You pretty much feel they weren't paying attention to what you said. This can happen in our relationships with students. As a teacher, it is important to listen with thoughtful attention, respond appropriately, and convey an interest in our student's thoughts. This shows them that their message is important to us, and that makes them feel valued. Students are very perceptive; they know when you are genuinely interested in what they have to say.

I coach a lot of new school administrators, and my job is to be there to support them in their positions. As much as I try not to, I've often stopped to realize that I'm talking about my experiences rather than listening to theirs. It's tempting to want to share similar personal stories, partly to let them know they're not alone and others have been in that situation, but also because most of us like to talk about our own lives. So, I need to remind myself of the W.A.I.T. acronym before each coaching session.

For those of us in education, there are many opportunities to learn from our students if only we can ask ourselves this question: *Why Am I Talking?* How often do we allow students to share their ideas and thoughts? Listening should be a major part of our job as educators. Whether it's listening to a student or a parent, we need to know their concerns, joys, fears, and desires and what's behind them. Sometimes, these are masked underneath anger or tears. It's important to peel back the layers to find the truth. To do that, we need to listen.

Listening reminds me of an incident that occurred with Molly, a kindergarten student. It was late May, and the school principal had just finalized the last class list for next year when he received a call from one of his kindergarten rooms. "Molly is throwing everything again. Can someone come down here and remove her?"

He knew what that call meant. Molly Brown was having an "off" day and couldn't control her emotions. The only way she knew how to express her frustration was to throw anything she could get her hands on: books, pencils, whatever. As principal of the school, he received these phone calls frequently, and usually, it was because Molly was mad about something a classmate did or said. These outbursts caused her teacher to interrupt her teaching to get help for Molly.

He picked up the phone and dialed Pam for support. Pam was an Intervention Specialist, and one of the two staff members their school had on-site from the Carson Student Center, a non-profit group whose mission was to disrupt the cycle of poverty and empower students. Carson had a contract with the school district to provide mental health services for students with behavioral and emotional challenges. They were lucky to have Pam on site full-time.

Pam quickly arrived in his office, and they hurried down to the classroom together. Pam was able to guide Molly away from the others, talk with her, and calm her down while the principal briefly spoke to the teacher about the situation.

In this case, Pam removed Molly from the classroom allowing Mrs. Winter to continue to teach the rest of the class. Then, as Pam listened to Molly's frustrations and talked with her, Molly was able to settle down and deal with her anger by using some of the tools Pam taught her, like deep breathing and counting to ten. Within half an hour, Molly was chatting with Pam and happily returned to her classroom, ready to learn. Several months of working with Pam had significantly reduced Molly's outbursts.

Having mental health services on a school campus is essential for the growth of the students. For decades, we've had counselors at the high school level, but that support should start in pre-school and extend through high school. Part of the on-the-spot intervention that The Carson Center provided was listening to students, showing they cared, and valuing the student's feelings. Molly wanted to be successful in school, but she didn't know what to do with her emotions, and when she would have outbursts, it interrupted her learning and the rest of her class.

Many traumas occur in the lives of our students, and when these traumas disrupt learning, the students can't access instruction. Teachers have the responsibility of teaching all their students. When one has a behavior issue, if someone is available to pull that student aside and talk to them, it generally diffuses the situation and allows the teacher to continue instruction.

Unfortunately, not every school has the luxury of a counselor on-site, so finding other resources on campus, such as another adult or peer who has a relationship with the student, can also provide a calming influence.

Everyone wants to be successful in life, but some lack the tools to help them cope with their frustrations. Through thoughtful and intentional listening by adults, students can learn coping strategies to help them develop their strengths and be more successful in school.

I guess there's a reason why we humans have two ears and one mouth. Perhaps we should think about that when we're around others, particularly in this environment of such divisive viewpoints. Trying to understand another's point of view is easier if we first listen and try to hear what they say, and we can't do that as well when we're talking.

> **"What every child wants to know is, Do your eyes light up when I enter the room? Did you hear me and did what I say mean anything to you?"**
> ~*Toni Morrison*

ENGAGE IN UNDERSTANDING YOUR STUDENTS!

"**You never really understand a person until you consider things from his perspective.**" *~Harper Lee*

$\mathcal{W}$hen Sophia threw her pencil across the classroom and yelled at her teacher, "You're the worst teacher in this whole school," she was sent to the principal's office. Rather than immediately chastise Sophia for talking about her teacher that way, the principal first tried to understand why she acted the way she did. In doing so, she learned Sophia was upset with her teacher for embarrassing her in front of the whole class by saying out loud, "Sophia, if you had studied for this test, you wouldn't have gotten a zero on it."

It doesn't mean that Sophia should not have a consequence for talking to her teacher that way, but a consequence that helps her learn more constructive ways to handle her frustrations has a better chance of resolving the situation. By taking the time to understand why Sophia acted the way she did, the principal showed her that she cared and valued her opinion. It's an important way to build trust with a student.

Our responses to challenging behaviors can be more effective if we are able to express emotional neutrality when implementing discipline. Emotional neutrality is about not taking the behavior personally. It involves understanding that although the behavior that is taking place may involve us, it is often about much more than just us, especially if the student has a history of trauma. Trying to understand a student and their behavior requires depersonalizing the behavior by asking questions to help us understand it. For example, what makes the student feel so unsafe that he/she must show this type of aggression? Is the student struggling with academic work that may cause him/her to feel vulnerable? Is the student battling with friendships that make him/her feel unwanted? Are their challenging home situations?

Students with unsupportive environments outside

of school often have defeating experiences inside of school. These experiences can build up over time and result in a reinforcing cycle of negative experiences between students and educators. Often, this causes educators to form negative feelings about certain students. Also, many times, the perceptions we form about students are based on what someone else has said or only from a single observation. They may be an unfortunate label placed on a student and not be completely accurate.

If we can depersonalize these negative experiences and try to understand better where the student is coming from, we can start to move forward in helping them change negative behaviors. Understanding the student doesn't mean we agree with their behavior or point of view. It means we are trying to see their point of view and validate their feelings. When we take the time to listen to students and try to understand where they are coming from, we can often break the cycle of negative feedback and begin to build trust with them. The student can then reorient their relationship with the teacher and the school.

I'm reminded of Monte, a third grader. He was tall for his grade, slim with curly black hair and big brown laughing eyes. According to his father, he always counted his toys at home, put them into groups, divided them up, and then rearranged them again. His dad said he could play like this for hours.

In the classroom, it was another story. Monte had difficulty sitting still and paying attention and was frequently out of his seat, talking to other students, disrupting the teacher's lessons, and negatively affecting his grades. Quite often, he would end up in the principal's office.

In the first few months of third grade, his teacher and his principal had several conversations about Monte. They discussed his need to move around in the classroom and how they could modify his surroundings. His teacher had tried many different strategies, but it was now November, and she was running out of patience with Monte.

The principal kept thinking about Monte. What made this kid tick? The district test scores had just arrived, and she decided to look at them. You can imagine her surprise when she saw that Monte scored in the 98th percentile in math.

The next day, she sought out his teacher.

"Take a look at this test score. Did you have any idea Monte was that proficient in math?"

"No, I'm shocked. He does do well in math when he sits still long enough to pay attention."

"Was he one of the students recommended to be assessed for the Accelerated Math (AM) program?"

"I never even thought of him. He's not the kind of kid who would normally qualify for that program. He's so squirrely in class."

Based on his test scores, they decided to recommend him for the next round of assessments for the AM program, which was designed to extend student knowledge in math and challenge their thinking. If he was scoring this high in math, they wanted to understand more about him and give him every opportunity available."

So, the next month, Monte joined several other third-grade students in their multi-purpose room to participate in the district assessments in English/language arts and math. It turned out Monte qualified as being academically talented in math. This meant that he could participate in the AM program once a week. His teacher was shocked when the principal shared this news with her.

"I can't believe I didn't see this about him. I think I was so influenced by his disruptive behavior that I never took the time to understand him. What happens now?"

"Let's schedule a meeting to share this news with Monte's parents. I think it would be important for Monte to be present when we tell them."

The next week, they met with Monte and his parents and shared the news. A huge grin spread across Monte's face. His parents hugged him; they weren't used to getting this kind of news from school about their son. The teacher and principal explained the program and how Monte would have a different teacher during his time in this new class, and the entire time would be spent doing math games and puzzles and learning new math strategies. They also discussed how this was a special opportunity, and everyone doesn't get to participate, so paying attention and following the rules and procedures was very important. Monte said he understood that and would try his best to focus and not disrupt the class.

Soon Monte began to blossom. He started to show more confidence in himself as a student, and he paid more attention in class. He began to ask questions when he didn't understand something. Amazingly, his academic success not only showed up in math, but his writing improved dramatically.

By getting to know more about Monte, they came to understand he was capable of being successful academically, and so did he. They learned that the illusion of who is academically talented is not always correct. Sometimes we need to dig deeper to get under the surface and understand what motivates a student.

"Everybody is a genius, if you judge a fish by its ability to climb a tree; it will live its whole life believing that it is stupid."

~*Albert Einstein*

RESPECT YOUR STUDENTS!

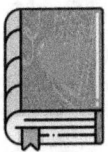

"**Give to every human being every right that you claim for yourself.**" ~*Thomas Paine*

*R*espect is not tangible.! It can't be seen, heard, or touched. But it definitely can be felt. It can be felt in the way a person listens to and affirms others. It can be felt through caring, kindness, politeness, and thankfulness shown to others.

What is respect? It's the regard for an individual's value or capacity. It's an act of giving consideration to others. It's the feeling of individual worth that you relate to somebody through your actions and words. I think about this often in my work in schools. In what ways do the adults on campus show respect for the students and each other?

During the Covid-19 pandemic, there were countless adaptations teachers made for their students. There were many things to teach students about distance learning: how to mute themselves, how to turn video off and on, and how to use the *Chat* feature.

Their learning environments were now their homes, and we needed to respect the many different atmospheres surrounding them. Teachers spent time on these things at the beginning of the shutdown so instruction would go smoothly. One area they couldn't control was the condition in the homes where their students were accessing instruction.

An example of this was in Hannah Long's second-grade class. She wondered why one of her students, Julian, always sat in the dark during class. She could barely see him because the room he was in had no light on. In class meetings, he engaged in the discussions, he turned in his homework, and she enjoyed having Julian in her class. He was eager to learn, responsive, and quickly caught on to new concepts, but his Google Classroom screen was always dark.

They had just finished the first week of school, and she decided she needed to ask him about it.

Hannah would talk to him during recess, but she was teaching subtraction at that moment. The kids were using small whiteboards to record their work. Julian was showing his whiteboard on the screen when a light suddenly turned on in his room. She could see someone else behind him laughing; it looked like it might be an older brother. Julian began waving his arms. His screen was muted, but judging from the expression on his face, it appeared he was yelling at the other person. This commotion disrupted her lesson as the other students focused on Julian's screen. When she looked more carefully, she realized he wasn't in his bedroom, at a desk, or at the kitchen table; Julian was in the bathroom, sitting on the toilet lid.

All the students' screens were muted, but she could see snickers erupt throughout her classroom. Soon, Julian disappeared, and his screen went blank. He didn't return to class for the rest of the day.

Hannah was concerned. She was sure he left class because he was embarrassed. He could have been crying and didn't want the other kids to see him. Had he been in the bathroom for all the other sessions? If so, that was probably why his screen was always dark.

Hannah was aware that Julian's mother had recently been jailed for a minor drug offense and that Julian and his brother and sister had gone to live with Grandma. But why was he in the bathroom for class? She would try to find out more about his situation.

When school ended, she found the vice-principal, Marcie, in her office. Hannah explained how Julian was attending class from his bathroom.

Marcie shook her head, "I'm not surprised. There are a lot of people living in that two-bedroom apartment. It's probably the only quiet place he could find. I've been talking with Grandma about another of her grandkids. Let me make a phone call home, and I'll get back to you."

Later that afternoon Marcie found Hannah in her classroom and explained there were fifteen people living in Grandma's two-bedroom apartment. She explained that not only were Julian and his siblings living there, but Grandma was caring for one of Julian's aunt's four kids and yet another of Grandma's daughters and her family were staying there temporarily while escrow closed on their new home.

Hannah couldn't believe it. No wonder Julian was in the bathroom trying to attend class. He couldn't find any other quiet place. There was probably not an inch of space where he could sit and concentrate.

She asked Marcie, "Do we have an extra headset

somewhere? And do we still have any of those tall tri-fold dividers the kids used in the Science Fair?"

"Good idea. Let's go check. That could at least give him a private space."

After rummaging through the school storage closets, Hannah and Marcie found a headset and an extra tri-fold divider. These would be perfect for him. He could find a corner of his apartment, put the headset on, and sequester himself behind the divider. Then, he wouldn't have to attend school in the bathroom. They contacted Julian's grandma and arranged for Hannah to deliver the materials to the house that afternoon.

Grandma greeted Hannah at the door; Julian was behind her. Hannah explained what the divider and headset were for and gave them to Julian. He immediately put the headset on, and a smile lit up his face. But soon it disappeared, and he looked up at Hannah.

"I don't want to go back to class and see the other kids. I'm afraid they'll laugh at me." Hannah paused; her heart melted.

"Julian, they won't even remember. With that headset on, you look like a jet fighter pilot ready for takeoff, and they'll think you're really cool." He grinned!

From that day forward, whenever Julian attended class, he wore his headset. The school ordered more headsets and tri-fold dividers; they wanted to respect the home environments of their students and ensure that no other student was forced to learn in the dark.

In a school setting, showing respect is one of the more important "lessons." It's taught through actual instruction on how to listen and be kind to others, but more importantly, it's cultivated through the actions of the adults on campus. Hannah recognized Julian's home situation, respected his predicament, and cared enough to take action to support him.

Remember the old sayings: *"Children learn more by what you do than what you say,"* or *"Actions speak louder than words."* And as W. E. B. DuBois said, *"Children learn more from what you ARE than what you TEACH."*

When we take heed of these sayings, which are more than just maxims, they become words to live by, words that we can take to heart and think about every day we're around students. If we ask ourselves, "What message am I sending to students by what I'm doing?" it prompts us to listen to our students and pay closer attention to our own words and actions.

Respecting students also makes me think of another situation. Eddie was a spunky, wiry third grader whose mouth never got a rest. One day he was in trouble on the playground for pushing another student so hard it caused him to fall into a tree and cut his lip. Eddie was sent to the office, reprimanded because of his aggressive behavior, and told to spend the rest of the afternoon writing an apology. The other boy was treated for his wound and sent back to class.

When the principal walked into the office to talk with Eddie, she saw him sitting on the bench, head down, balancing a blank piece of paper and pencil on his lap. He looked up at her and then lowered his head. She told him to go into her office and sit at the table. She had gotten to know him through their many visits together well enough to think that he wouldn't have pushed another student around unless he had a good reason. Eddie was impulsive, but he was also a caring kid. Before she talked with him, she needed to locate the Yard Duty Supervisor to see what happened. She found her in the yard and asked if she knew why Eddie pushed the other boy.

"I don't know why he did this," she retorted. "You know him, he's so impulsive, he just does these things."

"Did you ask him why he pushed Jason?"

"No, it all happened so fast, and I was concerned with getting help for Jason."

After hearing from her what occurred, the principal realized the Yard Duty Supervisor hadn't taken the time to ask Eddie for his side of the story. In her frustration to help Jason she hadn't listened to Eddie.

The principal went down to his classroom. She wanted to talk with his teacher to see if she'd heard anything more about the incident.

"I was just about to call you about Eddie," the teacher said. "Some of the kids told me that the reason he pushed Jason was because Jason was sitting on Tracey and wouldn't get off her. She was yelling that he was hurting her, but he wouldn't move, so that's why Eddie pushed Jason to get him off her."

The principal returned to her office to talk with Eddie. She told him what she had heard and asked if the story was true.

"Yes," he responded. "Jason was sitting on her, and it was hurting her, so I pushed him to get him off her."

They talked about how he could have handled the situation differently. Did he know why Jason was sitting on Tracey? Could he have talked with Jason? Could he have asked the adult on yard duty for help? It's a constant training, helping students learn how to handle their frustrations in a manner respectful to others.

Respect permeates the halls of a school, weaving its way into the fabric of the school culture. The behavior of the adults at a school has a direct impact on the environment at that site. Everyone on campus is responsible for showing respect for others, whether for teachers, parents, or students. It starts from the top and trickles its way down. Using a political term, we could call it "trickle-down respect."

"Respect people's feelings. Even if it doesn't mean anything to you, it could mean everything to them."

~Anonymous

ACTIVATE OWNERSHIP IN YOUR STUDENTS!

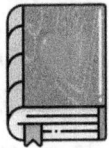

> **"The best teachers show you where to look, but don't tell you what to see."**
> *~Alexandra Trenfor*

$\mathcal{W}$e hear the term "Ownership" used frequently in reference to students. What exactly does it mean? The dictionary says it's "the state of being an owner." If we transfer that term into education, it means a student is the owner of their learning. We also hear the term "Agency" used a lot. Again, according to the dictionary, agency is "the capacity or state of exerting power." So, when combining these terms, giving students agency and ownership is showing them how to take power over their learning. As teachers, we can provide agency and ownership for students in many ways: through welcoming student voice, providing multiple learning opportunities, encouraging wondering, and allowing students to learn from their mistakes.

Part of ownership is student voice. For example, it's important to help students engage from the beginning when creating a classroom environment. Teachers can encourage student voice by asking them what they think. That creates an ownership of what goes on in the classroom.

My friend teaches high school biology. Whenever she tries a new technique, she asks her students how it works for them as learners. Did it help them access content? Did it help them analyze the material she presented and make sense of it? She wants their voice involved in the teaching strategies she uses. After hearing from them, her next step is implementing her student's ideas into her instruction. When we ask students for their opinions and then implement their ideas, it tells them we value them and what they have to say. For younger students a paper survey could be used showing their responses in emoji faces.

Over the years, we've discovered that not all

students learn in the same way. Do we provide multiple opportunities for them to share their perspectives? Not all students want to speak up in class, while others could easily monopolize the entire conversation. Some students thrive on working together in groups, while others are more productive when working independently. Do we provide different ways for them to share their thinking? Having students turn to a partner and express their ideas after hearing a presentation allows all to verbalize their thoughts, not just those who raise their hands and are called on.

One strategy for hearing from all our students is to have them respond in writing to a particular lesson. For some, writing can be a powerful way to put forth their ideas in a less public way than speaking.

Working on a project as a group or individually can also provide a different learning opportunity. When creating a product, students need to strategize and plan steps for what they will do to come up with the end result. They learn the give and take of collaboration. There is always that risk that one student in the group will be the "slacker" and let others do all the work, but isn't that also a learning experience— learning how to deal with that kind of situation?

When students have different ways to express themselves, which may be more conducive to their learning style, it promotes ownership and allows them to feel more in control of their learning. When we teachers vary our learning methods, more students become involved in class, their confidence increases, and they learn to drive their learning proactively.

As early as first grade, teachers can be the guide in letting students take the lead in their learning. For example, when teaching younger students writing skills, many teachers use their students' ideas to put together sentences and paragraphs as a group. When they record these writings on chart paper and post them in the classroom, it engages and motivates students as they see their own words on display.

We also learn from our mistakes. Helping students take ownership of their mistakes and understand them provides a wonderful opportunity for learning. As teachers, we can share our mistakes, what we did to overcome them, and what we learned from them. In her book *Mindset*, Carol Dweck states that developing a growth mindset in students helps them see that persistence and hard work can help them achieve their goals. When students fail at something and try again, they learn you don't have to achieve your goal every time to be successful. Babe Ruth, one of the best hitters in baseball, had a batting average of .342; that means he got a hit less than four times for every 10 times he was at the plate. It's those times in our lives when we fail, or things don't turn out as we wish that we learn the most from.

High school students can be encouraged to understand how their learning affects their lives. Do we provide opportunities for them to research when they want to learn more about something or someone? What better way to stimulate ownership than to allow students to delve into a subject they've chosen to learn more about? Do we encourage them to wonder how their reading connects to them? Tying the curriculum to everyday experiences brings lessons alive and makes them more than just stories from history or algorithms students may not see how they'll ever use. It connects learning and life, which our students don't always see.

I'm reminded of my conversation with Ryan, a high-school sophomore who shared a situation with me where he learned to take ownership of his learning. Covid-19 had just reared its ugly head, and the stay-at-home order was sprung on everybody almost overnight. His school was scrambling to pull together online learning since everyone would be quarantined in three days. Ryan told me, "I think I would've taken it more seriously in the beginning if I'd known what it was going to be like or even known what was going to happen. I really didn't know what to expect. Actually, I don't think anyone else did either. I know my friends didn't."

Things were going well for him in high school. After figuring out halfway through his freshman year how the system worked regarding grades, online assignments, and keeping track of things, he now felt a little more in control. Basketball season was ending, and he had played well, so he felt good about hopefully making varsity next year.

Then on March 16, 2020, his world turned upside down, along with everybody else's. Covid-19 was spreading more quickly than people thought and the governor declared a statewide shutdown. People could only go out for basics like food, and only essential workers could go to work. Schools started what everyone called "distance learning."

At first, they didn't know what was happening. Students were getting assignments online from their teachers and turning them in electronically. It didn't seem very organized, but soon, they got into a routine as the school put a block-type schedule in place. Teachers gave online lessons and assignments for students to complete during the rest of the week. Ryan told me sometimes he had to set his alarm early and sometimes his first class was later in the day. It was definitely different than what he was used to, and he didn't feel very connected. He turned in the assignments and did what was required, but didn't think he learned much. He said he was just going through the motions.

One day, he overslept and rushed to log into his Spanish class. He was waiting for the teacher to let him in when he got a chat message, "Ryan, would you please put your shirt on before you come into the class meeting." *Oh my gosh*, he realized he had just gotten out of bed and had forgotten his clothes. "Good thing I had pajama bottoms on," he said. He told me it probably wouldn't have been a big deal to the class. Most kids looked like they had just gotten out of bed with eyes still half-mast, messed up hair and no make-up on; they didn't care. They all thought this was going to last for three weeks, and soon, they'd be back in class.

Then, word came out that the quarantine would last until the end of May, and students wouldn't return to school at all that year. That was a huge disappointment. Ryan hadn't seen his friends for three weeks, and another month seemed like torture.

Basketball and football had started up, but they only had online conditioning. Somehow, watching a one-hour video of Coach directing squats and weightlifting wasn't very motivating.

He told me days started blending together; Saturdays were just like Tuesdays. After about a month, their parents began to feel sorry for them and let up on their restrictions. He was allowed to see his friends as long as they stayed six feet apart. They could get together in driveways, backyards, and on the beach when that restriction was lifted.

He thought seeing each other helped them get used to this new lifestyle. After all, they were going through it together. But he still felt something was missing. His friends and he agreed they weren't tuned in to their classes. But how do you make yourself care when this is going on?

One day, his English teacher talked to them in class. What she said had nothing to do with English but with their situation. She understood what they were going through and asked them three questions: "What was working with distance learning?" "What were the biggest challenges with it?" and "What was one step they each could take to make it work for them?"

He said they had the best conversation together as a class. Everyone had a chance to share their feelings about their situation, and they all felt heard. Then, their teacher challenged each of them to set a goal for themselves, something they thought they could attain that would help them engage in class and keep their learning alive. She asked them to also keep a journal of one new thing they learned each day in class.

That made Ryan realize his motivation wasn't going to come from outside. He needed to discipline himself and own his education. No one else could do that for him. He knew he'd never have this much time on his hands once school and sports started again. He should try and make use of it. He started paying more attention to his classes, not just to completing the assignments.

Ryan and his friends didn't know what school would look like in the fall and they didn't know when they would be able to return to play sports in the gym or on the field together. However, they did feel better prepared to take ownership of their learning. He thanked his English teacher for making that happen.

By encouraging student voice, providing multiple strategies for learning, embracing mistakes, implementing their ideas in the classroom, and asking probing questions, we give students agency to take charge of their learning. Research shows that students who take ownership of their learning are more effective at identifying and working toward learning goals, developing a sense of self-efficacy, and more often believe they are in control of their success.

> "Teaching students is an accomplishment; getting students excited about learning is an achievement."
> ~Robert John Meehan

EXPECT YOUR STUDENTS TO SUCCEED!

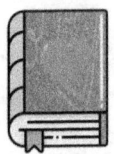

> "A master tells you what he expects of you. A teacher, though, awakens your own expectations." ~*P. Neal*

When someone expects you to be successful at something, do you think it has an impact on whether you succeed or not? Think back in your lifetime about a situation when a parent, teacher, or other adult believed you could do something. Was it to achieve your best time at a swim meet or to ace a test in Algebra? Whatever it was, how did that person's belief in you affect your success?

What did they do or say to cause you to reach your goal?

For many years, I have participated in non-profit organizations that award college scholarships to students. These youth are either in the foster care system and/or may be the first in their family to attend college. Ninety-nine percent of these scholarship recipients credit a strong adult influence in their lives for helping them succeed in school. So many, in their acceptance speeches, thank a teacher who believed in them. I remember when one recipient, Claudia, said, "My math teacher, Mrs. Evans, told me I was college material." No one in Claudia's family had ever attended college, and she never thought she would until her teacher made that statement.

However, many times, we educators don't follow Mrs. Evans' example and fall into the trap of lowering our expectations for students living in poverty, English learners, or family situations that don't support education. It isn't because we don't care. It's because we aren't aware of the profound effect our expectations, and the words we use, have on a student's success. We need to witness their story and have compassion for their situation, but not lower our expectations and think they can't accomplish what their more privileged peers can. We must never discount a student because of the conditions into which they are born. We need to be what Zaretta Hammond, author of *Culturally Responsive Teaching and the Brain*, calls a "warm demander—one who focuses on building strong relationships with students, then draws on that wellspring of trust to hold students to high standards of deep engagement with course content."

Think about this! Michelle Obama was raised in a small apartment in the South Side of Chicago, where her family lived with relatives, and she has accomplished so much. More than likely, Michelle Obama had a "warm demander" in her life, or maybe more than one.

Our job is to draw out the best in our students by showing that we care and believe in them. We can do this by observing and listening to them and asking them about their interests and goals. We can encourage them to try new things while letting them know it's okay to make mistakes as we learn from them. We should urge our students to express their ideas in writing, write about their experiences, and respond to issues of the day, which can be fantasy or non-fiction. We all have ideas and opinions about life and the world around us, but sometimes, students don't value the thoughts in their heads.

I recall observing a 3rd-grade writing lesson. The teacher had just given the students a class writing assignment, asking them to describe their favorite animal. As she walked around the room, she noticed Javier had not written a word on his paper. She approached him.

"Javier, what animal are you going to write about?"

"I don't know," he responded as he lowered his head.

"What's your favorite animal?"

"A tiger."

"What do you know about tigers?"

His head perked up; the beginning of a smile appeared on his face as he told her, "They're cats, they have orange and black stripes, they live in the jungle, they're fierce."

"Perfect, that's what I want you to write on your paper."

"Really, I can write that?"

"Yes, you know a lot about tigers, so now tell me about them in your paper."

He got to work, and when he was finished writing, he composed a beautiful story about tigers and their importance in the world. Javier didn't know that what he was thinking about tigers was worthwhile enough to write down in an essay; he didn't value his own thoughts. He just needed to know his ideas were important and believe he could express them. He needed to know his teacher expected him to be a writer.

There is a very tiny but powerful word we can use when encouraging our students—YET. It packs a powerful punch! Think about the impact of these two different sentences....

"You can't do that." Or You can't do that, YET."

There are two very different messages here. One is defeating, and the other is expecting success. That one little word implies something is achievable.

Imagine if someone had told Babe Ruth (George Herman Ruth) as a young kid that he wasn't a good batter. Would he have continued playing baseball? Would he ever have accomplished what he did? Would he ever have thought he could hit home runs? He may have just given up on baseball. Then again, if his coach told him, "George, you're not a very good batter YET, but I can show you some tricks to improve your swing because I know you can be a home run hitter."

The "Babe" would have heard a very different message from his coach—one that expected him to succeed and gave him hope that maybe he could hit a home run. Those words would have told him that with practice and effort, it was possible to achieve his goal.

In education, we must consider the messages

we're giving to our students. When they say, "I can't do this," do we help them understand they just can't do it YET? Do we assure them they're capable and then give them tools to accomplish the task? It helps develop a growth mindset in students if they think there is a possibility they can learn or achieve what's expected. We need to give them the message that if you keep working at this, you can learn it, and don't give up.

Our words matter more than we realize when dealing with students, and those words can have long-lasting effects.

This idea applies to adults also. When we suggested all teachers at our school hold class meetings with their students, as one way to get to know them better, two teachers were very resistant. They told everyone else it was a waste of time. After further conversation with them, I learned what was underneath their reluctance. One teacher told me, "I've never held class meetings before. I don't think they'll work. Won't the kids just be talking over each other? It sounds like chaos." Once they were assured they could first observe class meetings in action and then begin conducting them at a comfortable pace, they agreed to try. And you know what? Their classes loved it, and both teachers developed closer relationships with their students. They just hadn't learned how to do it YET.

That reminded me of when I was in a master's program at the university. There were twelve of us in class, and the professor asked everyone in the group to raise their hand if they thought they were good readers. Only six people raised their hands. I was shocked that just six us—all who already had earned their bachelor's degrees—thought they were good readers.

The professor then asked the six, "Why don't you see yourselves as good readers?" Without exception, each said they had been in the bottom reading group in first or second grade. Think about how long those people held that belief. All of them went on to graduate from high school, complete their undergraduate college degree, and now were in a master's program, so, obviously, they could read perfectly well. But each person still viewed themselves as a poor reader.

Think about this when you're dealing with students or maybe your own kids or grandkids and remember to let them know they just haven't learned it YET!

The power of this small word allows for success rather than defeat.

66 "My teacher thought I was smarter than I was, so I was." ~Six-year-old

STRATEGIES FOR MAKING MEANINGFUL CONNECTIONS WITH YOUR STUDENTS!

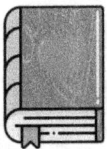

*H*ere is a compilation of strategies discussed in this book:

✔ **Pay attention to your Ratio of Interactions (ROI)**

- ROI means making a conscious effort to interact with a student more frequently when they are doing something appropriate as opposed to when they are doing something inappropriate.
- A good goal is 3:1: Three positive to 1 negative interaction.
- You may need to adjust this ratio up for your more challenging students.

✔ **Practice the "2 x 10" Strategy**

- From Christopher Emdin, Author and Educator
- First, select a student you are struggling to connect with. Engage that student on any topic for two minutes, then continue having those two-minute conversations about any subject for ten consecutive days. Emdin's research indicates there is a significant improvement in that student's behavior.

✔ **Conduct a Student Strengths Survey**

- Questions in the survey ask students what they see as their strengths and areas for growth, what are their dreams, etc.
- There are many samples of Student Strength Surveys available online, or you can prepare your own.
- The information provided can let you into the student's world and what is important to them.

✔ **Use the *W.A.I.T.* Technique**

- Think to yourself, *Why* Am I Talking?
  Should I be listening instead.

✔ Ask Students if Your Teaching Strategies are Working

- When you try a new technique, ask your
  students how it worked for them as
  learners. Did it help them access content?
  Did it help them analyze the material you
  presented and make sense of it? Elicit their
  voice in the teaching strategies you use.
  Then implement your student's ideas into
  your instruction.

✔ Provide Multiple Opportunities for Learning

- Provide multiple opportunities for students
  to share their perspectives. Not all students
  want to speak up in class, while others
  could easily monopolize the entire
  conversation.
- Have students turn to a partner and express
  their ideas, after hearing a presentation this
  allows all to verbalize their thoughts, not
  just those who raise their hands and are
  called on.

- Have students respond in writing to a particular lesson. For some, writing can be a powerful way to put forth their ideas in a less public way than speaking.
- Provide opportunities for them to do research when they want to learn more about something or someone.

✔ Encourage Students to Learn From Their Mistakes

- We all can learn from our mistakes. Helping students embrace their mistakes and understand them provides a wonderful opportunity for learning.
- YET is a very tiny word but it packs a powerful punch!!!!! Think about the impact of these two different sentences....."You can't do that." Or "You can't do that, YET!"

✔ Express Emotional Neutrality

- Our responses to challenging behaviors can be more effective if we are able to express emotional neutrality when implementing discipline. Emotional neutrality is about not taking the behavior personally. It involves understanding that although the behavior that is taking place may involve us, it is often about much more than just us, especially if the student has a history of trauma. If we can depersonalize these negative experiences and try to understand better where the student is coming from, we can start to move forward in helping them change negative behaviors.

✔ Leave Sarcasm at Home

- You don't know how a student will interpret your attempt at humor.

✔ Remember You Are a Role Model

- Educators are role models, whether we realize it or not. Students look up to their teachers and watch carefully how they handle situations.

RESOURCES AND REFERENCES

- "2 x 10 Strategy", Chris Emdin, Author and Professor at USC
- Peter Johnston, *Choice Words*, (Routledge; 1st edition,2004)
- Zaretta Hammond, *Culturally Responsive Teaching and the Brain*, (Corwin; 1st edition, 2014)
- Dweck, Carol S, Ph.D., *Mindset*,(Ballantine Books, Updated Edition, 2007)
- Denton, Paula, *The Power of Our Words*, (Responsive Classroom; 2nd Revised edition,2013)
- Poulson, Simon, Ph.D., *A Fine Balance: The Magic Ratio to a Healthy Relationship*, (Purdue University)
- Kaufman, Trynia, MS., *Building Positive Relationships with Students: What Brain Science Says*,(Understood.org)
- Leadership: Association of California School Administrators, *From Gatekeeper to Ally*, (May-June 2023)
- Coughlin, C., Resnick, J., & Sprick, J., Leadership: Association of California School Administrators, *Harnessing the Power of a Positive Ratio of Interactions (ROI Concept)*, (January-February 2024)
- Delizonna, Laura, *High Performing Teams Need Psychological Safety*, (Harvard Business Review August 2017)
- Platinsky, Miriam, *How a Welcoming Classroom Can Help Decrease Absenteeism*, (Edutopia, September 2023)
- Ferlazzo, Larry, *Response: Building Relationships with Students is the Most Important Thing a Teacher Can Do*, (Education Week, October 2018)
- Ed Trust and MDRC, *The Importance of Strong Relationships*

Between Teachers and Students, (The Education Trust, March 2021)

- *The Optimum Context for Learning: Drawing on Neuroscience to Inform Best Practices in the Classroom,* (Educational and Child Psychology)

FROM THE AUTHOR

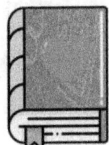

I hope the thoughts expressed in this book reminded you of the importance of getting to know your students, building relationships with them, and expecting them to be academically successful. It is easy with some students and much more challenging with others, but those are the students with whom we need to go the extra mile to make the connection.

Hopefully you learned something new in these pages that you can apply in your daily teaching.

I would like to thank all the educators out there who are making meaningful connections with students in their everyday work. You are making a huge difference in the lives of your students.

I would also like to thank my teacher friends who

patiently read these stories and gave me feedback, my friends in Nancy's Writing Class, and Nancy Henderson, who critiqued my work and kept me on target, my husband who was always supportive and honest, and my editor, William Gensburger who is not afraid to tell it like it is, which I greatly appreciate.

If you liked the book, I would love it if you would leave a review on the site where you purchased it. It helps other readers find the book and helps the author spread their message.

~*Jane Blomstrand,*
   July 2024

ABOUT THE AUTHOR

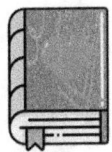

Jane Blomstrand is a retired educator. She has held many different positions in education including classroom teacher, Literacy Specialist, Elementary School Principal and Director of a Teacher Credentialing Program.

Currently Jane is coaching new administrators. She and her husband live in Northern California.

MEET THE PRINCIPAL: My Journey Beyond the Curriculum by Jane Blomstrand

Most of us have experience with school, either as students, parents, or teachers. However, few people have experienced walking in the shoes of a school principal. **Meet the Principal** is a collection of stories from one principal's experiences. These stories show the many intriguing challenges a school leader faces each day.

What Readers Say:

"**Meet the Principal: My Journey Beyond the Curriculum is a captivating journey into the heart of education,** offering a unique perspective from the vantage point of a school principal."

~ A. Morrison, Book Review - Glass Books

"This book was a fun and entertaining collection of stories of what educators deal with in and out of the classroom. It is an excellent read for anyone stepping onto a campus and especially those working with students. I couldn't put this book down and really enjoyed it! I recommend it to everyone!"

~ H. Asselin, Teacher - 5 Stars on Amazon

"Meet the Principal is a good book for all teachers and those dealing with school administration as the author shows the connection between the students and their families, teachers, and the curriculum in an engaging light. The stories are funny, sad, touching and tell readers what happens at a school beyond its curriculum."

~ M. Madhavan – 5 Star Book Review - Reader's Favorite

You can purchase the book on Amazon or at independent bookstores. https://amzn.to/3S13Cmo

ISBN: 978-1733245906.

July 2019,

310 Pages

Website: www.MeetThePrincipal.com

READER NOTES